YOUR KNOWLEDGE HAS VALUE

Mark Schauer

Repressed sexuality and drug abuse in Stevenson's Strange Case of Dr. Jekyll and Mr. Hyde

GRIN Verlag

Bibliografische Information der Deutschen Nationalbibliothek:

Die Deutsche Bibliothek verzeichnet diese Publikation in der Deutschen National-
bibliografie; detaillierte bibliografische Daten sind im Internet über http://dnb.d-
nb.de/ abrufbar.

Imprint:

Copyright © 2012 GRIN Verlag GmbH
Druck und Bindung: Books on Demand GmbH, Norderstedt Germany
ISBN: 978-3-656-46852-3

This book at GRIN:

http://www.grin.com/en/e-book/230260/repressed-sexuality-and-drug-abuse-in-
stevenson-s-strange-case-of-dr-jekyll

GRIN - Your knowledge has value

Repressed sexuality and drug abuse in *Strange Case of Dr. Jekyll and Mr. Hyde*

by Mark Schauer

Few stories that are over a hundred years old retain as much importance in the popular imagination as Robert Louis Stevenson's 1886 *Strange Case of Dr. Jekyll and Mr. Hyde.* Aside from the title characters becoming a shorthand description for a person who manifests a frightening bipolarity, the novel's gothic depiction of London remains the popular conception of the city during the late Victorian era. Though the story is commonly interpreted as a depiction of good and evil and the duality of man, *Jekyll and Hyde* is in large part a gothic allegory about repressed homosexuality and covert substance abuse.

Jekyll and Hyde has endured largely because the story's dual hero/villain was conflated with Jack the Ripper, the alleged perpetrator of a series of highly publicized murders of London prostitutes that began two years after the novel was published. The assailant, who was never captured, was presumed by the contemporary press to be, like Jekyll, a respectable man of the upper class who indulged his homicidal proclivities by night in the guise of a pathologically violent alter-ego (Cohen 3). The problem with framing the coverage of these murders within the *Jekyll and Hyde* narrative, however, is that Hyde was never portrayed as murdering a woman. In fact, women are strikingly absent from most of the story. None of the other major characters, from Jekyll to his long-time friends, are married, and except for the young girl he tramples and his female servant, Hyde is never shown associated with a female. Despite a predominately male servant staff, Jekyll's house is well-appointed: "Utterson himself was wont to speak of it as the pleasantest room in London" (Stevenson 16). Hyde's own quarters in Soho, the low class neighborhood which was the epicenter of London's gay sex trade of the era, were similarly, "furnished with luxury and good taste" (Stevenson 23). In 1886, this type of aestheticism was effeminate. Further, aside from being an unmarried middle-aged man who seems to associate exclusively with men of his own class in like circumstances, it is significant that Jekyll is only once depicted outside the house, a feminine sphere. The activity he was engaged in—sunning himself in the park—is similarly passive, indulgent, and feminine by the standards of the day.

Hyde's ultimate crime was the murder of Sir Danvers Carew, a member of parliament. The killing was witnessed by, "a maid servant living alone in a house not far from the river," who reported it took place sometime between "about 11" and "two o'clock when she came to herself." (Stevenson 20-21). The deadly beating was precipitated by the, "aged beautiful

1

gentleman" Carew approaching Hyde with, "a very pretty manner of politeness" (Stevenson 20). The text does not overtly explain why a member of parliament would approach another man in this manner at night in an area of town low-rent enough for a female servant to live in a house alone. Aside from the obvious explanation, there is quite a bit of suggestive language describing the scene to further buttress that Carew was soliciting sex: the maidservant witness was "romantically given," Hyde, "had once visited her master," and the murder weapon was a cane, a phallic object, which Utterson, "had himself presented many years before to Henry Jekyll" (Stevenson 21). When Utterson and Hyde first meet earlier in the story, Utterson tells him, "we have common friends," which makes Hyde nervous (Stevenson 15).

Everyone who sees Hyde invariably describes him as young, along with other descriptions that were coded female and other, from his footsteps ("light") to his voice ("husky, whispering"), his complexion ("dusky") to his propensity for "hysteria". Given his prominence in Jekyll's will, Utterson suspects that Hyde is blackmailing Jekyll for, "some old sin, the cancer of some concealed disgrace" (Stevenson 17). Utterson never considers that young Hyde could be Jekyll's illegitimate son, however, though illegitimacy was a common enough trope in commercial fiction of the 19th century, including Dickens' *Bleak House* and Collins' *The Woman in White*, both of which predated *Jekyll and Hyde* by decades. Is his failure to consider this possibility a result of his and Jekyll's religiosity, or the fact that he knows such a thing would be biologically impossible in Jekyll's case? What other relationship between two men could lead to one being the sole beneficiary of the other's entire estate?

If indeed Stevenson meant for Hyde to be interpreted as Jekyll's homosexual id unleashed by addiction to a psychoactive substance, it would have been quite impossible for him to say so directly in a commercial novel of the period. The pinnacle of Victorian England's sexual repression came with the Labouchere Amendment of 1885, a year prior to the publication of the novel, which outlawed all acts of "gross indecency". This was interpreted to mean sexual acts between men: In Victorian England, unnamed misconduct by a man was usually homosexual activity, and most of Hyde's hidden acts are ill-defined. Though middle class propriety prohibited the overt discussion of such matters in commercial novels, the London scandal press was not so muted. English newspaper readers had been exposed to sensationally lurid stories of upper class homosexuality since at least the 1870 trial of Ernest Boulton and Frederick Parks for, "dressing up in women's clothes and parading about in the company of young men" (Delgado 29). Remarkably frank 'autobiographies' like John Saul's 1881 *Sins of the Cities of the Plains* circulated in literary and upper class circles (Delgado 25). Oscar Wilde, author of *Jekyll and Hyde*'s literary cousin *The Picture of Dorian Gray*, was alleged to own a copy in testimony given during his trial for violating the Labouchere Amendment.

Homosexuality was also a common topic of English and French medical journals of the period, which Stevenson subscribed to and read with avid interest. *Jekyll and Hyde*, "resembled contemporary medical case studies in its form and structure, but its core idea may also have originated from medical literature" (Stiles 879). Though Stevenson denied it to reporters during his lifetime, the testimony of his widow and, "striking correspondences between Stevenson's work and case studies in French and British popular and medical journals during the 1870s and 1880s" suggests he was also influenced by this source (Stiles 881). Early considerations of drug addiction were also published in these venues, and that Jekyll is a substance abuser should be readily apparent to the modern reader versed in the general popular conception of addiction. To change into Hyde, Jekyll is dependent on an unnamed psychoactive substance. Across the narrative he builds a tolerance to this substance, needing higher doses to maintain the same effects. He engages in behavior he wouldn't dream of while not under the influence of the substance, and repeatedly and vociferously denies the extent of his dependence to himself and his friends. When he runs low on the substance, he goes to desperate lengths to acquire more, including impressing his estranged friend Dr. Lanyon into his service. "Jekyll's appeal to Lanyon is characteristic of the victim of addiction who, in turn, victimizes others by manipulating their loyalty, affection, or sense of obligation and duty to personal advantage" (Wright 260). Further, "the victim's preoccupation with his addiction leads the addict to create a ritual world by which the psychological strength of his addiction is magnified, (such as when) Jekyll's egomaniacal pride of accomplishment in his miracle of chemistry is indulged before his horrified colleague Lanyon" (Wright 256). Jekyll is clearly dependant on this substance.

From a purely medical standpoint, the novel represents the ascendance of internal medicine, which is arguably the most groundbreaking and least considered aspect of the work. This is embodied by the laboratory in the rear of Jekyll's property, "the building which was indifferently known as the laboratory or the dissecting rooms. The doctor had bought the house from the heirs of a celebrated surgeon; and his own tastes being rather chemical than anatomical, had changed the destination of the block at the bottom of the garden" (Stevenson 24). It could be said that, "the surgeon who was Jekyll's predecessor," (Stevenson 41) in a literary sense was Victor Frankenstein, another gothic doctor of ambiguous sexual orientation.

Works Cited

Cohen, Ed. *"*Hyding the Subject? The Antimonies of Masculinity in *The Strange Case of Dr. Jekyll and Mr. Hyde."A Forum on Fiction*, Volume 37, Issue 1/2(2003-04).

Delgado, Anne. "Scandal in Sodom: The Victorian City's Queer Streets." *Studies in Literary Imagination*; Vol. 40, Issue 1 (2007) 21-36.

Stevenson, Robert Louis. *The Strange Case of Dr. Jekyll and Mr. Hyde*. Oxford: Oxford University Press, 2008.

Stiles, Anne. "Robert Louis Stevenson's Jekyll and Hyde and the Double Brain." *Studies In English Literature 1500-1900*; Volume 46 Issue 4 (2006) 879-901.

Wright, Daniel. "'The Prisonhouse of My Disposition': A Study of the Psychology of Addiction in Dr. Jekyll and Mr. Hyde." *Studies in the Novel*; Volume 26 Issue 3, (1994) 254-67.